DARK LAKE

Dark Lake

Kathryn Kysar

Loonfeather Press
Bemidji, Minnesota

Cover art and graphics, *Leaves Floating on Dark Lake* by Marlon Davidson
First printing 2002
Printed in Canada
ISBN 0-926147-14-5

This activity is made possible, in part, by a grant from the Region 2 Arts Council through funding from the Minnesota State Legislature for RSV, healer of hearts

Acknowledgments:

These poems previously appeared in the following magazines and collections:

Communitas: "The Poet's Muse"

Dust and Fire: "Idaho Potatoes," "Juna Speaks to the Newborn Moon," "Wanting to Dance with the Bride," and "You Are a Man"

Lake Songs: a collection of broadsides from Loonfeather Press: "Postcard from the Prairie"

Midland Review: "Contemplating Flight"

2001 Minnesota Poetry Calendar: "Ilsa's Inventions"

2000 Minnesota Poetry Calendar: "The Insomnia House"

1999 Minnesota Poetry Calendar: "Postcard: Midnight at Dark Lake"

Mikrokosmos: "Fishing," "Lobsters in the Trees"

Painted Bride Quarterly: "Emily's Cat's Kittens"

Permafrost: "Jealousy"

Piedmont Literary Review: "Halloween"

The Talking Stick: "Escape from Paradise, Iowa," "After Vietnam," "Crossing Cultures," and "On Your Brother's Imminent Death"

I am grateful to Norcroft: A Writing Retreat for Women for feeding me while I was pregnant and to Forecast for a public arts affairs grant that provided time for writing potato poems. Thanks to Bill Borden, Marlon Davidson, Janis Leona, Fiona McCrae, and Nancy Michael for reading the manuscript in its early forms and to Kate Lynn Hibbard, Susan Steger Welsh, Anne Piper, and Bonnie Flaig for telling the truth about the latest poems. My sincerest thanks to Patricia Conner and Betty Rossi for their time and care in editing and preparing my manuscript for publication.

Table of Contents

Leaving Paradise

Hanging Out with the Boys

The Sky Whispers Its Forgiveness

Bodies of Water

Leaving Paradise

Escape from Paradise, Iowa

We are afraid of nothing.
At the diner,
you order a burger,
a grilled cheese for me.
We tell bad jokes,
pour salt on the table.
The waitress glares at us,
our clothes too tight,
my lipstick too red
for this small town.

This is the summer
of anger and beer.
We know everything:
how each blade of grass turns in the wind,
why the sunlight glints off the pool,
the shining of streetlights on black pavement,
the darkness of the lake at night.

At the bar
you say I am as Nordic
as blonde hair, these big bones
under the sheet of my skin
a frame for your thoughts.
I am the only one smoking.
My breath peels into the air like waves.

We have nothing in this town:
a beat-up Mustang,
a few songs on the jukebox,
the torn cover of a book you never read.
When we get in the car,
you pass me another beer.

We are scared of these random roads,
the small towns passing,
the gas tank nearly empty.
My head on your shoulder,
the eight track stuck again,
we're gonna drive this dirt road
all the way to Kansas City.

The Poet's Muse

I am only a small goddess,
soon to be replaced next year
by a corn god, a wheat king,
yet I have this magic with you;
I hold the hangman in your deck of cards,
your statements written on small napkins.
I know how the stone falls from your tree of monkeys.
I send to Cyprus for nude bodies, anxious
to remove this old skin, these false robes.
Disgusted, you want to leave and walk in alleys, ruins,
but I won't let you, practically tying you to my wrists with rage.
Yet I, the Flora of the story,
wrap your wounds with oil and bits of cloth
containing words of pity from Sappho,
who bleeds her heart for men like you.

The Pregnant Wife

She is growing daily, bigger
and wider, astoundingly, like a balloon.
Not just her stomach, but her hips, her thighs, her breasts.
She barely recognizes her body anymore.

She fears she is an empty husk,
an empty shell, a fragile fruit
with no seed, no pit, no center.
She longs to hear the baby
speak to her in kicks or flutters.

She draws pictures of tall round women,
skinny legs, long arms, bellies bursting
like surprise boxes full of jelly beans and M and M's.
She draws pictures of a woman with the belly
full of a reclining fetus, lines of gold
radiating from the center of the bodies.

She tells the children
she cannot swim with porpoises,
for they will hear her two heartbeats.

She eats and sleeps
a shell, a vessel, a container
on a sacred journey.
She looks at her mother now
and understands.

Jealousy

The flies are thick in this small room.
I cook fish over a sputtering fire.
We have no wood and cook with moss, grass
that smokes in this thin ocean air.
You say I don't appreciate your fine fingers,
that love means no golden ring, no silver chain.
But I've seen those girls
come to you on the streets,
their eyes like fishing lures,
their mantra, your name.

You are no sheepherder, no carpenter.
You are a fisher,
nets large enough for ten porpoises, twenty women.
But you catch nothing. I gather the nets.
I count yesterday's fish,
placing them in waxed brown pots from Syria.
I traded no daughter for you.
I have small tools I saw skins with.
In this dim light, my fingers are cold.

Wanting to Dance with the Bride

White: the silhouette of hair, shoulders, the flow
      of the gown against the cathedral windows
      steaming in the August Superior sun,
White haze on the big lake, white clouds,
White cake with almond filling,
White gardenias for the mothers,
White carnations for the teenage nieces
      with nose rings, purple hair, and clunky shoes,
White for the flash of the friend's camera bulb,
White for the teeth of the smiling groom,
White for the napkins, the thick paper of the guest book,
      the ostrich feather-plumed pen,
White for the baby's breath in the bride's hair,
White for the porcelain cups filled with coffee,
White for the cream, not the bluish tinge of the skim milk,
White for the aprons of the matrons who serve the buffet,
White for the scuffed shoes of the three-year-old flower girl
      as she strews petals on the lawn,
White for my blank face,
White for the sheets of my empty hotel room bed,
White for ignoring how he ignores her,
White for her hope for children,
White for his absence in her bed at night,
White to make me blank, uncaring,
White for transcendence,
White for wanting to dance with the bride.

After Vietnam

I have no memories of hell
or the times you wrapped
your legs round mine.
I've wished you dead,
not chained to bamboo,
your ears red welts
from mosquitoes and lice.

The war is over.
I hold this wedding ring
to water, almost letting go.
Our gardener brings roses.
His hands, small birds,
flutter like florist paper.

He tells the children
"All homes are shells,
all children pearls."
The sea inside me rises.
You rattle in my brain,
a pebble, a pearl,
within my skull.

On Your Brother's Imminent Death

It will all be over soon,
the black cars in the rare Kansas rain,
your mother leaning on the thin shadow
of your father.

You are curled
in the peace of our blankets,
dreaming the tinges of pink
that outline stars,
the lines of orange
creeping under the door at sunset.
I move toward the warmth of your back,
hold your curved body in my arms,
and whisper into your sleeping ear,
"It won't happen."

Fishing

Let the line hang loose in your hand,
feel the heat of the sun on your bare skin.
You are far away, relishing
the idea of an unknown jungle, thinking
yes, this is how the tree evolved and
no, this is not the place of my ancestors.
You may be the last person on earth,
everything you know bombed
because of Kirvograd
or a small village in Lebanon.
How will you snare your life,
the minnows running out, the radio dead?
Calling frantically into the woods,
you are surprised to see
your children and wife running toward you,
hot dogs in hand, a doll in your daughter's arms.
You are relieved but remember nothing.
Take the fish off your line.

Contemplating Flight

Hunched within his soul was a crow. The man, too, hunched inside his huge body of bacon grease and lard. She had learned to make the bed around him as his bones dissolved, but his breath falls easily now, a bird about to land. Each day, a cupped hand, extends itself—the possibilities of petunias, warm milk, the soft curve of her breast—yet he does not move, listening to the crow's songs, his instructions on flight. Someday soon he may spread the wings within him, but she tugs in him, a bird, a beast within his soul.

Halloween

This night
is a weave of lies.
This night is a towel
of blood, the smoke
of burning leaves.
There are apples in the bowl,
pennies for the smaller children
who come as ghosts, small spirits
in sheets that wind in the wind.

We light the pumpkin
we carved last week in the park.
It has caved in, the mouth
shriveled, toothless, and small.

Do I hate you or myself more
I say when the doorbell rings.
You sit on the toilet
making small circles under your eyes.
I hide in blue sheets, a walking bedroom.
Cleopatra and these sparkles,
these red lips,
are nothing you want to touch.

Crossing Cultures

It is not a seam well sewn.
Against the fallen hues of the autumn sky,
you spread your fingers: and this line
means long life. We straddle our bicycles
along the side of the road, poplars
shading the slanting afternoon sun.
It is a beautiful fall day in Beijing,
and I cannot run my fingers
through your tight black hair.

Inside the cement school building,
it is dark and cold. The electric light burns.
Our hands, dry leaves, brush slowly.
The wind blows carefully copied translations
on thin white paper from your desk.
My tea grows cold. You pick at a small blue thread
on your jacket. Silently, I turn and leave.

Your Man

He is not the type to share his jacket.
At the lake, the dog barks at rocks.
He says, "A lower form of life."

We stand in the wind,
lean against the car, drink beer.
He lectures me on socialism and Roosevelt.
He has the perfect plan for revolution.

We are mothers with soft and fleshy middles.
We lean on the kitchen sink and whisper
through the chicken, through the broccoli
what he cannot hear.

You Are a Man

A woman wants to be a man. She has taken over your side of the bed, wears your ties, and is now asking to take out the garbage. You nod, say sure, not minding all this until she stops doing the dishes. Your friends start asking questions, say, "Janey used to be such a cute little thing." Her friends wonder if she's gone gay.

Janey counts your ties like spring tulips, separating them into shades of orange, gray, and brown. "That's Greek Avocado," you say as she puts one in the green pile. She laughs at your pettiness, your arrangement of cologne bottles on the dresser.

She buys you an apron. In May she brings you flowers. She has grown taller, legs longer, shoulders broader in padded jackets, her humor cutting and smutty. She tells you about the new lockers at her gym, what her secretary said that day. When she tells you you're getting fat, you start to cry.

You take to drinking wine in the day, vacuuming the house at 3:00 a.m. Finally the headaches become too much. The doctor tells you it's nervous tension, but you don't believe him. You feel yourself shrinking, the dishes piling up. Tonight when she demands sex in a strange position, you give in, wishing you were a man again.

Hanging Out with the Boys

These poems do not tell the truth.
I make up the names, the lies
as I lie in bed at night
counting the cracks in the ceiling.

They are the boys in the band,
boys at the concerts in dirty t-shirts and leather,
their blonde hair long as the tasseled tops of corn.
I could tell these boys more
than they know about music,
but they think I am only for darkness,
the warmth needed after the show,
letting me into their motel rooms
where secrets uncurl like tongues.
I am like a guitar, tall, curved, but soft.
I make beautiful sounds when they touch me,
my neck long and straining.
I know the way a song must press lips,
the way a voice must crawl
the back of a throat to a scream,
the air smoky, thick
with things I shouldn't know.
If the radio was on,
I could sing.

I dance until my breath is steel,
until the backs of my calves
are hemp knotted tightly around bone.
We dance in front of the stage,
me, Donna, and that black girl.
We dance alone, for ourselves, for them,
offering our frenzied bodies only to those on stage,
my focus his eye, his focus my hips.
I am all want, all gone, consumed
in the beat, the loud ringing in my ears.
My body frees itself in the dance
I have practiced so many times in front of the mirror.
But it is not the same dance.
It is for you.

Michael,
I don't know really who I am.
I am a girl who ...
Who what? I am a girl
who is bad at math.
I am a girl who likes to draw
pictures of birds and pine trees.
I am a girl who likes to go to the ocean
and sit in the cold wet sand waiting.
I am a girl who secretly sings along
with the radio. I do many thing secretly.
I creak the lengths of the floorboards
with my bare feet, my dry skin peeling
into the slivers. I welcome pain.

For the Fourth of July,
Donna and I took her mother's car,
bought air mattresses,
and drove to an obscure point
far north on a rocky beach
and floated all day, our skin
red as the lobsters we dreamed of eating.
That evening we had the best food:
rare steak stolen under jackets
that looked ridiculous in July;
stewed tomatoes, hot and slightly
spiced; watermelon, the black seeds
in pink flesh that matched our own.
I rubbed a slice
across my arm to cool the skin,
each hair bumping up.
But it was the Noxema
we rubbed on each other's hot backs
that soothed, concluded the day,
as we fell asleep side by side
on her mother's double bed,
dreaming of nothing but
lake water and stars.
I wish they would stay away forever.

Michael,
I don't have enough thought
for all this conversation.
Your letters bombard me
like my mother's demands
to clean the house.
I cannot give you freedom
or flight, a chain
of letters to lead you to me
like Rapunzel's hair.
I can give you nothing, only
the few pictures I draw.
What do you want me to draw?
Winged seeds as they fall in the autumn air?
The slanted angle of the world
through the warped glass of the front window?
My mother's silent tears?
I draw nothing.
I send only the scent of my perfume
in an envelope that you will think is empty.
But look inside, open it wide.
In those dark seedless corners
is my trust.

If I stole that money
from your lingerie drawer
and boarded a Greyhound tonight,
you'd never know. Mother,
I am ready to leave this house
of sick dreams, unwilling
to play the fool in your nightmare.
I can no longer say, "Yes,
he shouldn't have left you.
Yes, he should have sent you the money.
Yes, he'll be sorry for it."

I will be my father, my mother.
I will walk out of this house,
a tall woman with a large shoulder bag
full of important music and clothes
and head straight north
where your dreams inside me will freeze.

I have cut my long hair.
I took the thick heavy strands
that hung like a curtain around my face
and cut them off, huge chunks at a time.
Mother says I look like a refugee
from Auschwitz. Donna stared,
her lips slightly parted as she passed me
in the hallways with her cheerleader friend.
We are like two refugees parted during the war,
and now, when the war is over, we no longer
recognize each other.

This highway is flat and filled with trucks.
We try to wave to the drivers
from our dirty Greyhound window,
but the tinted glass makes us look
like seaweed floating in an aquarium.
Our waving arms sway and float.
I count the numbered metal posts,
close my hands around my head
and try to sleep. The bus is cramped, jiggly.
There are lights far off,
and I wish I could see land passing,
the burnt grass, the colored shield of the sky,
but everything looks gray from this fishbowl.
I turn and sleep.

I hate the small wood houses here.
At home, our houses are dug deep, planted
with thick roots that must last
through the winter, big houses
that are dark in the summer and cool.

My mother's house is a museum,
the light dim and dusty,
prismed through buffet glass
like the faintly rusted water
from the pipes below.

I never knew my grandmother,
only heard stories of her accented voice
and ornate hairpins.
I study old women,
their voices cool as water,
their lips dry as hot schoolroom air.
I scrape their faces with my eyes,
my fingers running
this soft cheek,
that downturned mouth,
this white hair.
How many nights
will it take to unsmooth this face?
How many disappointments make a line?
I think of the pictures on the piano,
their burnt yellow faces strong
in the hesitant light.

Donna,
let's never get old,
captured in some frame
to yellow over the years.
May we dance forever
in the strong bare light of your bedroom,
the lace curtains parted like our lips.
We lift legs and feel the strength of our blood,
the strength of this old wood floor,
above air, above wood, above air.

Woke up this morning to discover snow, the grass
covered with thin layers of ice, unable to breathe,
matted down to the earth. That is how I felt
our first year here: the snow kept coming,
piled so high we dug tunnels in the large mounds
beside the street. Those dark tunnels' icy floors
were black from boots and fuzz from winter coats,
the snowsuits that scraped against them.

By January the tunnel went almost all the way
around the block, and our mothers could never find us
deep in the cold wombs with our flashlights.
I was happy then, huddling with the neighbor boys,
our bodies smashed against each other
like piles of secrets that layer my thoughts.

Now winter means silence, staying indoors
to read Mother's magazines. This silence is cherished
like the small china doll in my mother's buffet cabinet,
the pile of rosary beads beside her chair.
I comb my hair a hundred strokes,
a winter princess, my skin icy and white in the mirror.
My hair is so long now I can cover my face,
with a slight turn of the head,
let down the curtain of hair.

I hear my mother in the kitchen,
and I know I will go down and help her bake,
the smells of almonds and cloves floating up the stairs.
We will be silent, our four long arms kneading dough
in deep ceramic bowls, our yellow aprons
covered with flour. We will be silent
and knead like kittens nursing at their mother.

When I was little, I used to make people, spending hours
on the sugar hair, only to wail
when they came from the oven puffed,
the girls indistinguishable from the boys.
My mother would hold me,
my mouth filled with her floury apron strings,
her cotton sweater wet from my tears.

Perhaps I will remind her of this now,
and she will turn from her bowl and hug me,
remembering that there is something very small within me,
afraid of dark and snow.

The Sky Whispers Its Forgiveness

Postcard from the Prairie

The silence, a wine of regret, is a finger
of open fire creeping across the prairie.
She forgives with the fragility of snow,
inhales the steaming cloud of coffee
like an angel or a whore
and forsakes the blueness, the trees.
Her skin dances above her, vibrates
as it exhales the distance,
which smells like her father's pillow.

The fissure of her bad fortune
has a dark taste. The water beyond,
a sliver of warm lake, undulates
with the sleep of the shadows of dreams.
See the empty sky, the broken blanket,
the black bird of desolation, the finger of fire.

Father, your black shoe breaks
the snow, the water, the moon.
Her smoke—inhale, exhale—fogs
the trees near the lake, the sunlight
barely concealing, barely cracking through.
The blue horizon shatters.

Sylvia's Potato Poem

Who is she following with eyes closed?
The sky has been swept with a wide brush.

The girl—Sylvia—races home from school
to see the ewes lying in the field like fat woolly potatoes
peeled and washed by distant clouds,
the white wool rising in the rain.

We were playing.
Death moved quietly in the barn.
When she was eight or nine,
Julian, the violin man, told us
secrets in the stove-cold air,
his brown nose an Indian mound of red clay earth,
his skin dry and smooth.
He said a dog eats a crab.
He said potatoes smell of pine in moldy cabins.
He said I deliver ice. Wolves sing from the mountains.
He said there's smoke over my mother's grave.

By night it is all so different,
but I know the potato is the secret.

Idaho Potatoes

I don't know if the story is true: during the Depression, Grandpa was a tenant farmer in Idaho. Each winter morning, Grandma gave Virden and Ardis a hot baked potato. They walked to school down the flat Idaho roads, powdery snow blowing against their cold pink cheeks and frosted eyelashes, their mittened hands holding the prayers of steamy potatoes. To keep warm, the children spoke of pleasant things: singing in church, eating summer apricots in the neighbor's orchard, whispering to the chickens in the damp, dark henhouse. Virden imagined proudly riding atop the vibrating tractor, its hum loud enough to make men shout. Ardis worried: she had to stay clean, she couldn't play in the trees. Only alone in the hen house as she collected the eggs was she happy, each stolen brown orb damp and warm and pulsing against her skin like the morning's baked potatoes.

At the school's playground, children ran and screamed. Ardis stood on the side of the trampled snowy field while gangly Virden ran, toes pointed in, ran with the pack of skinny boys, joking, laughing, and shoving. In her perfect Shirley Temple curls, in her starched cotton dress and wool stockings, in her worn coat buttoned up to the neck, she waited for the older girls to ask her to play. She waited for Mrs. Youngquist to call them in to class. She waited for lunchtime when she could join her brother on the rough wooden bench in the corner to eat boiled eggs and cold potatoes, the white middles flaking into their mouths, the browned skin crispy, cool, and comforting on a cold winter's day.

Potato Harvest: A Photograph

They stand in the furrowed field,
dried up weeds gracing the mounds of dirt,
men to the side, women in white,
freshly starched dresses, one holding a swaddled baby.
They are finished with the harvest:
potatoes in burlap sacks on the back of the wagon,
six bushel baskets in front. The woman in the center,
holding herself apart from the others,
wears the biggest white dress with frills around the arms,
a bow tie, and a straw hat with a fake flower.
Stern and proud, this is her harvest. She is the owner, the boss.

They are all in a line: the sacked potatoes
on the wooden cart, the six horses, the people in front.
Four men with hoes stare at her, almost snickering.
Behind the woman in white is a blur of movement,
a ten-year-old girl gussied up against her will
and dragged unwillingly to her grandmother's harvested field.
There are two younger women, one with her hand placed
jauntily, seductively on her hip (she's no farm girl);
her younger sister looks on, pretty, sweet, and proud.
Off to the side are two older women,
one with a baby, and an old man with a long beard,
poorer relatives from Sweden, indebted
to the woman in white. The hired hands look on, amused
by this picture-taking of the potato harvest.

Photographs from Beijing

These are the pictures.
Here I am arriving.
Notice the neat cut and uniform color
of my hair. Here I am at the Great Wall.
My lover did not take this picture,
though you may think so.

This young woman framed
by a brick open window?
Her boyfriend took our picture
as she held her plastic bag tightly
against her peeling red vinyl jacket.
She stood stiffly formal, close enough
for us to see her unbrushed teeth,
smell her breath.

Distance is only time, not space,
and tonight as I make fish with my Chinese family
and practice saying "ue,"
you will be a trickle in my thoughts,
a scent on my fingers,
a picture above my desk,
a trace of time.

Things I Learned in Denmark

Don't put 20 krona coins in public phones:
they don't make change.

When eating eel,
place the bones
around the edge of the plate
in a circle, then make a cross
to save yourself from a sailor's death.

Don't put stamps on postcards.

When opening a bottle-capped cola,
gently rotate the bottle
as you pry the lid off.

Meat and potatoes sustain the soul.

I do need a walk daily.
I don't need coffee before bed.

Children in all countries like bears and farts.

It's good to dance with students
to old Beatles tunes while drinking beer.

Sailors wear yellow rubber raincoats;
little girls wear red.

Bring wine to everyone's house for dinner.

Do point to your hometown on the map.

Take naps whenever possible.

Expect rain.

Coyote Speaks in Riddles

Etch the formula outloud
with your tongue.
Under the misting world,
ruin the stone, forgive
the broken doves, move
the sordid clouds, break
the green staircase.
Sleepily, find the alley, turn left,
then utter the star-broken words
"absence" or "sleep" or "withdrawal."
Your own lucidity departs, echoes
the shadowy residue of afterthoughts.
Question your history. Discover
the limits. Find your answer.

A Key Is an Island: A Weekend in Florida

1. Sunday
In the Everglades after the hurricane,
I hike in thigh-high water, fearing
the white-toothed jaw of the alligator.
A great blue heron bursts upward:
feathers against air, an audible flapping of wings.
The tall pines like Dr. Seuss trees,
long and skinny with a puff of green feathers on top,
the sun hot on my reddened skin.

2. Saturday
The canoe paddle dips silently
in the dim green water, inches
through the sawgrass swamp,
three feet of water and a limestone bottom.
Minnows dart from the canoe paddle.

3. Saturday Night
Our foil dinner: potatoes, onion slices, mushrooms,
and baby carrots steamed in the damp wood fire,
sirloin burgers cooked on the grill.
Faces flicker in the firelight.
A black crow grabs a potato peel.
Green feathery pine needles make mosquito-feared smoke.
The tent walls are damp with dew and humidity.

4. Sunday

Hiking alone, wading through the hurricane's waters,
a drying alligator in the sun,
the fearsome stubby legs and toes,
I chant *alligator, crane, osprey, great blue heron, egret.*
I am a mammal, belong with brown, furry animals in cold woods,
not in the sawgrass swamp of poisonous snakes.
I cannot run in water,
I cannot climb these thin pine trees.
I do not belong here, I do not belong here, I do not belong.

Emily's Cat's Kittens

The kittens died last night
small, perfect, and wet,
tiny claws, mouths closed,
strangled by umbilicals.
Interbred,
there was no instinct
left in Emily's cat.
She stared at them,
licked a bit,
but took no real interest,
had no understanding.

Emily is scared, of monsters,
people, the dark. I know a lady
who has poison, she says.
Maybe Monica was poisoned. Maybe
she didn't know her babies
because they were poisoned.

The witch did it.
She is the one prowling
the basement windows, knocking
branches, breaking twigs.
She creaks the floorboards,
makes the dogs howl.

Emily has created a religion
of resistance. She clutches
her fear, fights for it.
Emily, let's read a book about
faeries. No, she says, no.

Ilsa's Inventions

Deprived of a picturesque childhood,
Ilsa invents possibilities:
snow without the absence of stars,
delightful china plates of fudge
with mounds of fresh oranges and fruit,
a new name meaning "summer flower,"
a window that always shines with daylight,
awakening to the smell of cocoa and oatmeal
brought directly to her bed by her own maidservant;
Paris, Paris, Paris, Paris;
gifts of small intricate wooden toys
hidden in the attic in delicately wrapped
packages by her portrait-perfect mother;
globes that show all the oceans and reflect the sunlight
in a dimly lit library filled with English children's books
to be read aloud by a full-time librarian
with a delightfully squeaky voice like a mouse.
She invents Greek ruins for the backyard
to wander amongst when she feels lonely;
comets and eclipses every evening at 8:00
to observe through her own telescope;
a cote of doves to fly within her gardens.
All of this to forget the violent aching madness of her heart.

Lobsters in the Trees

My family was on vacation
when the campground tank pump broke.
We ate four whole lobsters,
gluttonously sucking
the meat from the shells.
My sister dreamt that night
of lobsters in the trees,
wind blowing branches, claws,
as we lay in the back of the Volkswagen,
my legs kicking into her nightmares,
the storm blowing darkened leaves against car windows.

You cannot sleep,
my legs kicking into you.
You dream you are a lobster,
and I, a lobster archeologist.
I pick apart your shell,
numbering each crack, crevice, and splinter.
Rolling over, you go outside and pace,
breaking branches at irregular intervals.
Each time I try to crack the neck at the base of my skull,
the shell of my brain,
you answer.

Another Postcard from Chinook

The wind on the prairie moves
straw-like grass. It undulates
against the crackling dry air.
It is not winter.
She is in the attic inventing
the whispering ghost of her father.
In the almost aching silence,
the movement of birds outside the window
shatters the peaceful madness,
but the light can't break through
the tattered shades,
the piles of forgotten pink insulation.
She climbs down the broken, creaking
stairs to stand and face the prairie.

Coyote Addresses Science

Tell the beads
of the chromosomes
like a rosary, Father.
Skip the wave-flattened rock
out onto the foaming,
frothing lake;
forget the icebergs
in your golden,
panther-like mind.
Feel the stars shine
upon your feet.
The sky whispers
its forgiveness.

Bodies of Water

Poem for Dark Lake

1

The old Indian man rose from the lake
and took my almost sleeping hand.
I too was Anishinaabe. We rose into the sky
above the misty, humid clouds,
into whiteness. There, his magnified hand
holding pine seeds, he said,
"Sprinkle these around the lake."
The seeds poured from his hand to mine.
I scattered them around the edges of the lake.
The dream ends.

2

I swim out
into the cool water,
my swimsuit cumbersome,
keeping me from joining the fish of the shallows,
the bubbles of oxygen that rise to meet my each step on shore.

I swim out
past the calm water
into the rippled current to the ominous peninsula
haunted by lily pads and broken floating wood.
I pause. Three pine trees
on Lee and Dolly's land sprout straight and tall
from the white birch forest.
They are the pine trees I planted in my dream.

3
The woman across the lake
makes sweat lodges for her children.
They learn ceremonies of tobacco and thanks.
She is a fierce wolf mother
and dislikes my city smells.
I show her the peonies,
tell her of my dream. She nods.
I am awake. The sky sprinkles seeds of rain on us.

The Pregnant Wife Forgets

She reads
your brain gets smaller, shrinks
with pregnancy, the words, thoughts,
images, and fluids migrating
to the thighs, belly, and breasts.

She forgets the stamps
on her party invitations, forgets
the driveway of her best friend,
calling lost from a convenience store
half a mile down the road.

But she never forgets the grocery list:
grape juice, spinach, noodles,
grated cheddar cheese. On impulse
she buys chocolate milk, hard salami
she eats hidden in her car, forbidden.

At night she floats
free from her huge body,
breathing lightly
to the dreams that turn inside her belly:
images of strollers and red-haired boys,
babies that pop out like miracles,
her body, thin and taut, restored.

During the day, she forgets,
but at night, at night, she remembers.

The Insomnia House

In the seventh moon of her pregnancy,
they cannot sleep.

The dog sighs and scratches.

The baby flips like a porpoise, all bubbles,
its internal, nocturnal splashes
hitting the sides of her belly.

Her husband turns his ironing-board back to her,
his buttocks slightly curved,
his skin firm, cool, and smooth.

Her belly, moon-round and glowing,
pulls on muscles and ligaments as she turns,
resettles her hip into new alignment.

The dog sighs and scratches.

She gives up, and, pushing with both hands,
raises her body to standing and lumbers,
each foot thudding on the wooden floor,
toward the bathroom.

The moon shines in the window.
The dog turns and sighs.

Midnight at Dark Lake

Dive off the dark dock
silhouetted in moonlight.
Arch forward, then away
from the full moon. Slice
through the feathery lake mist.
Swim past the weedy undertow
into the clear water,
the top layer still warm,
cool underneath.
Crawl with four limbs over the surface,
your body skimming just below the mist.
Add the round creamy white moon,
the rhythm of your breath,
and Orion, the messenger,
always watching over you.

November

Dried brown sticks and marshland stems
encircled with thin crusts of ice.
Sun slants from the far horizon.
Frogs burrow deep in the lake's mud.
The bear turns in his last moments
of wakefulness. The land is sleeping.
Snow, the thankful anesthesia,
comes to cover the brittle land, a blanket
of sparkling crystals reflecting the sun's light.
Small birds hop along the icy crust
making fork-like prints. Mice skitter
along the side of the field. Trees glimmer
with their new adornment of white.
Bear smiles in his sleep,
a peaceful rest, a happiness, a renewal.

The Stairs

Usually, he stands
at the top of the carpeted stairs,
arms held tight by his side,
little hands curled into fists,
eyes turned to mine,
as he waits for his ride down,
indicating his wish with his whole body.

But tonight, with Daddy and dog
downstairs, his will overcomes his fear:
he plunges, head down at the turn,
legs first for the long stretch,
half crawling, half sliding,
down at a rapid pace.

Horrified, I stand frozen below him,
ready to break the imminent fall,
but he keeps going, propelled by will,
propelled by fearlessness
to the bottom,
where he runs to the dog
in that toddler gait
for a joyous, celebratory
lick on the face.

The Pregnant Wife's Husband

She is growing daily,
her breasts full and round,
punctuated by tight red nipples,
her stomach, hips, and thighs
voluptuous, ambitious, and warm.
This is not the woman he married,
but her body responds to his,
and he buries himself in her softness.

In the evening, he eats vanilla ice cream
dripping with strawberries from last summer's bounty
mounded in black ceramic bowls.
He eats in the dark on the couch, sucking
the sweet icy delight from the spoon,
almost imagining himself in her womb.

At night, he dreams of her round rump,
her luxurious breasts.
His body, long, lean, and taut,
he holds her as she grows outward
and into him.

Juna Speaks to the Newborn Moon

I barely breathe.
I still want wings about my head
and night to live in our dark houses.
I want to run away with a band of soldiers,
those red threads secure
to the empty expanse of my own death,
still smoky from your deep gray angora birth.

During the day, I forget
the knotted violet vein of trials,
the blood of innocent children,
the dead and leaning grass.

But at night, at night,
it is all so different:
the liquid possibility of my waist,
and the skin-salt taste of swallows
under the eaves. My head on your shoulder,
we leave this dark forest of confusion.
I do most everything for you. And I'll be gone.

The Pregnant Wife Eats Dirt

It is gray everywhere: coal soot
on the eaves, rain changes to sleet
changes to dirty white snow. We
have nothing to eat but potatoes,
turnips, and bread. I crave
green: braised kale, spinach,
even shredded cabbage.
The sky is pregnant too—full
of round clouds scudding the sky.
I barter the ring for a cabbage,
make soup, but it doesn't satisfy.

One night, when they are all asleep,
I touch the tip of my tongue to a sliver of coal,
but it is gritty, dusty, and black.
The next day, the children napping,
I take a tablespoon into the garden,
dig under the icy layer of snow to the gray clay dirt
beside the fence. I put the spoon to my mouth.
It tastes of aluminum, feces, and clay pots.
I put my spoon in again, lift it to my lips,
then hear my neighbor splashing her wash water
out the door. I stand, smooth my apron,
slipping the spoon inside the pocket,
wanting the sky to darken, the moon
to open up and swallow me, feed me
rocks and gold, minerals and diamonds,
all the hardness in the world
to make this soft baby grow.

Bodies of Water

Elsie wrote
on the newspaper lining
of her sewing cupboard
mothers are the ocean
their children swim in.
The baby inside me burps, flips,
confirming her truth. The mother
is the ocean and the boat, the rubber raft
and the assailing storm, the water their bodies float in.

Marlon's cells
are rebelling, sewing nebulous flesh
into shadowy, unconfirmed masses.
He awaits the tests as these cells
flourish at night in the dark,
sapping his energy, using his fat,
growing these strange fruits.

The baby converts my dinner
into flesh, into eyes and nose,
brain cells and bone. She takes my energy
plus apple juice to make blood.
She takes the car song of her brother
and makes movement, a leg or hand
hitting the sides of uterine walls
to the internal waves of sound.

Marlon,
I am eating a pumpkin pie for you tonight.
I am eating Caribbean rice. I am drinking whole milk
and dreaming of breakfast with toast and butter.
I am converting this food into energy into mass
into cells. I wish I could give you some.

What is it like to live in a home of water,
to breathe and drink the fluid of mother ocean,
buoyant and salty and clear?
I lie curled in the bathtub at night,
the lights turned low, mineral salts in the water,
the womb within the womb,
a mother becoming an ocean.

My neighbor tells me stories of Elsie:
Elsie plants a Haralson apple tree at age 98;
Elsie's scraps of scribbled sewing paper;
the night she sits on her porch during a storm,
the huge elm crashing down, its leaves
brushing her screen windows, her roof.
I always wanted to see a tree falling,
she said calmly, in awe, in wonder.
Perhaps my time has not come.

Marlon is pale and accepting;
he has cleared his heart to calm.
Remission: he stitches words into paper with paint.
Perhaps my time has not come.
The ocean inside him rises, a cleansing water
of peace. He wakes from the dream,
sips a glass of water, and breathes.

New Year's Day

Skiing beside Superior, silent
except for the rhythm of our breath.
Our feet slide forward in long, gliding steps.
When we reach the campsite,
I collect the firewood,
you set up the tent.

At dawn,
brown sticks thrust through sandlike snow,
gray water fades into cerulean sky,
and there is no way of telling,
no black line on the horizon,
no marking between sea and sky.

Sister Poem

The autumn sun drops its orange waxy dots
on the lake, and the geese fly
up—larger than my sister thinks
they should be. She is gone to California.
I did not get a chance to say good-bye, and now
the silence eats the long afternoons.

She called these death bells,
the ones with the little blue flowers,
hummingbirds darting in and out.
Those brown-haired girls at school
chased away the birds, their light
feet falling heavy in black shoes.
The birds would scatter then disappear.

Brow, her dog, lies on the braided rug
and dreams of God's colors:
a Noah's ark, a multihued robe.
Brow feels her absence too. Brow feels
these afternoon shadows twist. His legs twitch.
He runs in his sleep. He cannot be hemmed in.

Twilight is filling the sky—
it is hard to see, like a cloud
of dark humidity descended. Our thoughts
are drifting, Brow's and mine, as we take
our evening walk, and, as if dreaming,
we think we see you on the far island of the lake.
Like Jesus, we can see you, yet you're so far.

Kathryn Kysar's poems have been heard on A Writer's Almanac and published in many literary magazines including Great River Review, Midland Review, Mizna, Painted Bride Quarterly, and The Talking Stick. A winner of the Lake Superior Writer's and SASE poetry contests, Kysar has received fellowships from the National Endowment for the Humanities, Norcroft, The Anderson Center for Interdisciplinary Studies, and Banfill-Locke Center for the Arts. She teaches at Anoka-Ramsey Community College in Minneapolis.